SPACES IN BETWEEN

Collection of Poems

by Gil Saenz

Printed in the United States of America.

Library of Congress Control Number: 2021945787

ISBN	Paperback	978-1-68536-033-7
	eBook	978-1-68536-034-4

Westwood Books Publishing LLC
Atlanta Financial Center
3343 Peachtree Rd NE Ste 145-725
Atlanta, GA 30326

www.westwoodbookspublishing.com

This book of poetry is dedicated to all my relatives, friends, co-workers and associates who have given me so much encouragement and support.

TABLE OF CONTENTS

SPACES IN BETWEEN 1
SUMMER NIGHT REFLECTIONS 2
DREAM JOURNEY 3
THE ASCENT 4
APRIL SHOWERS 5
FLOWING MEDITATIONS 6
SUNSET MOOD 7
RAINDROP MEMORIES 8
FANTASY JOURNEY 9
THE VERY BREATH 10
FOR PEACE AND HARMONY 11
DESTINY 12
BEAUTY DREAM 13
THE SOURCE 14
AUTUMN STORY 15
BECKONING MOONBEAMS 16
WHEN LOVE WENT AWAY 17
LOOKING FOR HER 18
TWILIGHT 19
AS TIME PASSES 20
MOODS UNLIMITED 21
THE POET'S DILEMMA 22
FALL COLORS 23
GIFT OF THE PRESENT MOMENT 24
BLUE SKY THOUGHTS 25
ABOUT LOVE 26
DOWNRIVER MOON 27

BECOMING 28
COMPUTER GENERATION 29
RIDING ON A RAINBOW 30
HIDDEN ROSE BUSH 31
MIRACLES 32
FREEDOM OF SPEECH 33
HOW GOOD OUR LIVES MIGHT BE 34
RELATIONSHIPS 35
LAVENDER 36
SPRING THOUGHTS 37
HOPE 38
RHYTHMS 39
MOONLIGHT ON BISHOP PARK 40
AUTUMN LEAVES 41
DREAMS OF TOMORROW 42
HOW BEAUTIFUL 43
RARE MOMENTS 44
WHAT IS ETERNITY 45
SWEET SIXTEEN 46
AUTUMN FIRST LOVE 47
LOST INTERVALS 48
GRACE 49
POEMS OF LIFE 50
RAINBOWS 51
CITY SNOWFALL 52
CONTEMPLATION 53
WORLD TRAVELER 54
INCOGNITO 55
CAN I WRITE THIS POEM? 56
SPRING'S AMBITION 57
POETRY MAN 58
STARLIGHT REFLECTIONS 59
BLUE FANTASY 60
BLUE MIST 61

COLORFUL FIRMAMENT 62
DREAMING OF LOVE 63
EARLY MORNING STILLNESS 64
EDGE OF A FANTASY 65
FLOWER OF NEW LOVE 66
AUTUMN BREEZE 67
THE HAUNTED BACHELOR 68
NATURAL IMPRESSIONS 69
LILAC MAGIC 70
LISTEN TO THE WAVES 71
DREAM COME TRUE 72
LOVE FANTASY 73
LOVE IS NEVER A CLICHE 74
LOVE OPENS EVERY DOOR 75
LOVE PORTRAIT 76
MARIA AND THE MOON 77
MEDITATION 78
MEMENTOS 79
MIDNIGHT RHAPSODIES 80
THE MYSTIC 81
MYSTIC AVENUES 82
NIGHT WISH 83
OUR CREATOR 84
POEM OF BEAUTY 85
POEM SONG 86
REMEMBERING 87
REVERIE 88
FOR HEAVEN 89
SAYING GOODBYE 90
SOARING SPIRITS 91
STAY WITH ME ALWAYS 92
STRANDED IN TIME 93
TIME AND FOREVER 94
TWILIGHT BLUE 95

TWO HEARTS 96
WORDS OF LOVE 97
WHEN PATHS CROSS 98
COURAGE 99
A POEM A DAY 100
OTHER POETRY BOOKS BY GIL SAENZ 103

Preface

"Spaces in between" refers to all the odd moments in our lives when we have a chance to think things over. It is usually a time when we're waiting for something or someone at the plane terminal, or the train station, or the doctor's waiting room. Maybe we might be waiting in a long line at the super market. If we could examine and be aware of what we're thinking at these times we could be building our own "Spaces in between," or in other words, the important parts of our lives. Poems are many times all about
just such moments or spaces.

Gil Saenz
June, 2002

SPACES IN BETWEEN

The time went by so slowly,
While he sat there in the wating room.
Only minutes had actually passed,
Yet it felt like many hours had gone by.
Each of these times of waiting;
When he waited to board a plane,
Or waited for a taxi to arrive,
Or waited in the supermarket line
Made his mind wander and think
Of many things, even daydreams.
He would create whole new scenarios
Of what could and would happen.
What he thought about and how
He felt during these waiting periods,
Or spaces in between was significant,
And helped determine the quality
Of his life.

SUMMER NIGHT REFLECTIONS

The hot summer night thick with humidity
Brought perspiration to his forehead.

He looked out into the darkness
As he sat on his front porch.

He imagined many events in his life
On a make believe screen just out
There in the darkness.

Loves, triumphs, joys, defeats and sorrows,
All rolled by on the projection screen
Of his memory.

DREAM JOURNEY

Wandering through his unusual odyssey,
He finally arrived at a different shore
In the shadow of time,
And bending with the wind.
Exotic and nearly bizarre,
Many of his experiences had been
Like pieces of a dream.
Searching for the gifts of the angels,
And exploring in the sea of tranquility,
Passion, romance, and music
Had all been within his grasp.
Instead while spinning the dream,
He had finally come to enjoy
The simple music of nature,
And how beautiful
Is the park in the city.

THE ASCENT

In a few minutes time
We had ascended very high.
Above the many fluffy bright
White cottony clouds,
The roaring jets and
Contrasting quiet
Of the other passengers
As they waited in anticipation
To reach our cruising altitude
Were all concentrated as one.

We had arrived at Heaven's gates.
Only the angels and saints
Had been priveleged to witness
And to gaze upon
All this elevated splendor
And beauty that foretold
Of the glory of our Creator.

APRIL SHOWERS

Gray, drab and dreary,
It had been raining forever,
Unceasingly.
The raindrops gained
Momentum as they
Started to come down
More forcefully.
Filled with shining wetness,
The little drops appeared
As thin long columns of water
Until they hit the ground.
As they collided
Wih the concrete sidewalk
They created round silvery puddles.
It was so familiar
Yet so different and unique.

FLOWING MEDITATIONS

The light reflected upon the slowly,
Flowing water that was pouring down
In straight sheets but in a wavy manner
On the graded wall in the large vestibule.
Little diamonds of light and water
Created other worlds, other thoughts,
And other feelings all within.
Each little shining gem transported
My imagination to another universe,
Another world, and another time.
The wall of flowing waters had become
The wall of flowing meditations.

SUNSET MOOD

He saw the afterglow
Of the sunset last night.
It was all orange, yellow,
Golden and white.

It reminded him
Of many things.
Of how time continues on
And of what it sometimes brings.

The colorful afterglow
Appeared as a small
Part of eternity
As it streamed along
The horizon endlessly.

Something for sure
That he would never outgrow,
Was that sight in the sky
Of the shiny golden glow.

RAINDROP MEMORIES

Nightingale, that's what she was to him.
Misty fog was all that remained of her memory.

As the rain came down in a staccato rhythm,
It sounded like little pellets hitting the porch steps.

The constant tapping of the raindrops
Brought back still more images of his former love.

She could be like rain, refreshing and cleansing.
Her love had given him sunshine and life.

Now the pelting raindrops were washing away
All the old story of their former love.

FANTASY JOURNEY

All the clouds below were folded over
Spreading for miles and miles.
They appeared as fluffy, white cotton.
The huge jet plane traveled so rapidly,
The clouds seemed to move and change
Their shape and appearance.
Bright sun and blue sky
Made a clear contrast of the heavens.
It was the material for a daydream
Of imagining what would be in store
When we arrived at our destination.

THE VERY BREATH

It was a very fine moment.
It was the very breath.
It had made all the difference.
Two full years had passed
Since everything took place.
Now all that remained
Was a broken heart
And a sad face—
He had forgotten
To bring the ring.

FOR PEACE AND HARMONY

Tell the people about the good news.
Tell the people about the Lord Jesus.
Tell the people to lose their blues.
After all, He said "I have come so that
You might have life and have it
More abundantly."
"The greatest commandment is love."
If only people had not lost their
Christian bearings along the way.
Many more people would be working
For peace and harmony today.

DESTINY

Destiny was a pretty little girl,
With shiny black hair, fair skin,
Sparkling dark eyes and a beautiful
Easy baby's smile.
I looked down at her as I walked by
And she looked at me.
I thought to myself,
Destiny has smiled upon me.
How true.

BEAUTY DREAM

The blue twilight sky
Draped over the large band
Of full-bodied healthy trees
With small curly tops
Filled me with a nostalgic
Longing and indescribable wishes.
These feelings arose
As I had stopped to regard
This view of natural beauty.
I had a sense of time
That passes away and yet
Is also always the same.

THE SOURCE

The real source of all life is almighty God
He is the Uncreated Creator of all things
Both visible and visible.
It is mind-boggling to contemplate
This Source who is the Ultimate Reality.
Faith which is belief in the unseen,
Compels us to wonder in amazement
On this almighty, omniscient Source
Of all sources.
It is truly astonishing to realize
The tremendous greatness and power
Of this supreme Source
As we consider our own smallness
And our dependency on It.

AUTUMN STORY

The music of the wind
Brushing the leaves
Of the trees,
Made it all begin again.
All the memories
Came rushing back,
And started to unfold.

This particular season;
The wind,
And the familiar bouquet
Of the flowers,
Together recalled the story
Of all that once was ours.

It transpired a long time ago,
When we were very young
With lots of life yet to go.
Our own personal autumn
Was still very far away,
But then, we enjoyed ourselves
And those golden autumn days.

BECKONING MOONBEAMS

A strong wind
Forced the waters
To make the waves higher
Out on the sandy beach.

The light of the full moon
Reflected on the many
Shiny ripples and waves
Giving a sparkle to each.

It was all so much like life,
Going by with a lot
Of flash and sparkle,
Beckoning us to enjoy
And take advantage
Of everything within reach.

WHEN LOVE WENT AWAY

Love had flown away.
All the little tricks and deceits
Had finally taken their toll.
Now the road was strewn
With many sorrows and tears.

Maybe love would return one day.
The parties involved
Would have to return to their senses,
To be true to themselves.

Let love walk in again.
Let paradise and happiness
Shake hands and be friends.

LOOKING FOR HER

Looking for that matching someone,
Trying to locate the other part of his soul,
The lonely days and nights of his solitary life
Reminded him how much he wanted to be whole,
How much he needed a partner.
He was looking for her, his soul mate,
Wishing to be fulfilled.
The more he searched, the less closer
Did he seem to come,
The more his efforts were nil.

TWILIGHT

Turqoise colored sky, twilight,
Tinged with orange to one side,
Your beauty is almost always
Manifested each night.
You were meant to be praised
And give inspiration,
But many miss you
For lack of interest or inclination.
And yet there you are again.
Natural beauty, twilight,
For all to enjoy and admire,
Rosy-blueness or shiny fire.

AS TIME PASSES

Our life is but a tiny droplet,
In the ocean of eternity.
Tossed back and forth
In this vast body of water,
We try valiantly to swim,
To be competent.
Mostly, we learn by doing,
As time goes by.

Fleeting seconds, fleeting minutes,
Hours, days, weeks, months and years,
Our perception of time as moving
Leaves a very strong impression upon us.
We observe the clock and become older.
As time passes we also pass.
Time and motion are closely associated
In our minds and psyches.

MOODS UNLIMITED

Perfectly lonesome, that was the way I felt.
Time had brought matters to a head.
Although cheerful and happy sometimes,
Being in sync proved to be twice as hard.
The places were up high in the air,
And my moods were slowly getting there.
Just think and be happy I had been told.
Suddenly every day was okay.
The important word was 'our world.'

THE POET'S DILEMMA

The poet must take the omniscient view,
But many feel that it would be better not to.
Instead they feel he may not know
As much as he is saying so.

The poet expresses so many things,
The reader wonders how his imagination
Seems to have wings.

He can ponder microscopic life
Or he can travel to the ends of the universe
Where the stars and planets are rife.

If he doesn't proclaim what he feels inside
Some may feel that he has something to hide.
Each poet finds his own voice,
When he writes his words he must always
Try to express a suitable choice.

FALL COLORS

Gold, yellow, orange and brown,
Are some of the colors of autumn.
Rusty toned leaves blow around
In small concentric circles
Of the deserted playground.
On certain trees the golden leaves
Sparkle in the afternoon sun,
As they dangle from the many branches.
The large manicured lawns appear
As green carpeting covering all.
Blue skies, white clouds
And the many shadings of green
Are all on the master canvas
Of the Autumn season.

GIFT OF THE PRESENT MOMENT

As I look past the boundary
Of this life toward eternity,
The inherent mystery and magic
Of each passing moment
Glows ever more brightly,
Full of joy and wonder
Rich in potential,
Rich in meaning
Is this ever fleeting,
Yet ever present
Moment.

BLUE SKY THOUGHTS

There was no limit to the sky.
Endlessly, it went up and up, even
Farther still from the light blue space
All the way to dark blue,

Past the birds,
Past the clouds,
Past the airplanes,
Past the stratosphere,
And the ionosphere,
The blue sky went on
Beyond all boundaries,
To the infinite and eternal.

ABOUT LOVE

Romantic love is as tempting
As a luscious dessert.
It comes with hope and dreams,
Pleasures, joys and sometimes hurts.

It has sweet daydreams,
Pleasure tasting moments,
And enticing promises,
Why else would we take the plunge?

Matching hearts and matching spirits
Produce the music that we feel
When we're under its spell.

The ecstacy of romantic love
Drives and compels us to search
And search,
Hoping to find a love so real.

DOWNRIVER MOON

In the jet black waters,
A single moon beam
Had been sliced into many
Small dancing white waves.
Each bobbed back and forth
All in a long row of shiny lights.
The white wavy slices reveled
In their own sparkle
And natural novelty.

From the platform of water's edge,
Dimly flashing lights were
Visible in the distance
Along the Canadian shoreline.
From the bank of Bishop Park
The many lights out on the black river
Were flashing their warnings
To approaching ships and planes.

BECOMING

The spirit of each person has a chance
To grow and mature within the pure
Potentiality of this world.
We must all learn to live in the spaces
Of ourselves and of time.
We must nourish our spirit first.
Go with the flow is more than just
A current saying, it is an important
Attitude, or frame of mind to cultivate.
We must live at a reasonable pace.
We must learn to listen to the silence
Within ourselves that is always present
But not always easily achieved.

COMPUTER GENERATION

Computer generation,
It is filled with much sophistication.
Bits, bytes, programs, and concatenations,
Software, hardware, PC's and Office Automation,
Facts, figures, database, trends, online reports,
They're all the latest business sensation.
It's not the answer to all our problems,
But it has entered all facets of our daily lives,
It has so many different applications.
It has even begun to decipher the genetic code,
To unlock some of life's mysteries,
Much to many people's consternation.
While it has caused the loss of many jobs,
Which were menial, boring, and repititious,
It has created a large new industry of jobs
Which are computer related, highly technical,
And leave room for much exploring for the ambitious.
Computer generation, it has made a quiet revolution.
It has modernized our nation.

RIDING ON A RAINBOW

Catch a ride on a rainbow.
Know the brightness
Of the freshly clean,
Powder blue sky.
See the soft rich colors
Of red, green, yellow and blue
In the long, striped, arched band
Flowing across on high.
The long wide band
Flows and bends down
Near where the pot of gold
Waits with glitter all around.

HIDDEN ROSE BUSH

The hidden rose bush
Was never seen or
Admired by anyone.
Yet God nurtured
The beautiful bush
With many roses.
Like all creation
The hidden rose bush
Manifests the love,
Power, and the beauty
That goes unseen
And unadmired
In many parts
Of the world
Each day.

MIRACLES

Each miracle that we observe
Whether it is large or small
Is God, our Father's way
Of showing us that He is
The almighty Creator of us all.
In a flash of an instant
His mysterious, awesome powers,
And supreme, omniscient spirit,
All become readily apparent.
We realize that God possesses
Tremendous, unlimited qualities
Of which we humans are not blest.
While faith is reconfirmed,
Unbelief is sometimes jarred into
A return to the previous faith.

FREEDOM OF SPEECH

Don't silence the voices,
Though you may dislike the face.
Don't silence the voices,
We're all part of the human race.

Don't silence the voices,
We need to understand all sides.
Don't silence the voices,
Allow wisdom to be at high tide.

Don't silence the voices,
We all must join the fray.
We need all the help we can get.
In this modern age and day.

Don't silence the voices,
Diversity is an important key.
After all, freedom of speech,
Is one of our greatest liberties.

HOW GOOD OUR LIVES MIGHT BE

From the gift of my imagination, it occurred to me,
While contemplating the beauty and nature of a tree,
How unusual and how rare life might be.
The tree simply stands there without much motion.
It soaks up the sun, the air, and the rain
Without very much commotion.
It grows and thrives without using a lot of energy.
If we humans could live our lives like that,
To effortlessly live and grow and develop,
How good our lives might be.

RELATIONSHIPS

Are getting acqainted.
coming closer.
small talk.
breaking down barriers.
sympathy and understanding.
genuine affection.
friendships.
a smile, a tear,
And a laugh.

LAVENDER

The unforgettable beauty of lavender
Occurs in both the earth
And in the colors of the sky.
It is an aromatic flower,
As well as part of the many changing
Shades of the daily heavens on high.
The creamy color in the sky—
Color of dawn—
Is quickly there and then is gone.
Light, violet, lavender
How unique is its special glow.
Colored in nature in light lilac,
Amethyst, and airy purple indigo.

SPRING THOUGHTS

Spring flowers blowing gently
In the wind,
You help restore
My peace of mind again.

Calm gentle wind emanating
From the southerly flow,
Your warm and cool breezes
Bring back memories of long ago.

Refreshing rains which help
Clean the air,
Are one more way
Mother Nature shows us
That she cares.

Tulips, lilacs and roses
Spring up in many gardens
That I pass.
And I know that Spring
Is here again at last.

HOPE

Hope is like
The first rays of sunshine
At the dawn of a new day.
It is like finding the answer
Whenever we go to pray.
Hope is like having been lost,
And now being able to find the way.
Hope is confidence and inspiration,
Going forward and not feeling dismay.
It is encouragement and promise
In finding the light that shines
At the end of the tunnel's way.

RHYTHMS

Rhythms of life,
Rhythms of love,
Rhythms of laughter,
Rhythms of the seasons,
Cycles and tempos,
Beginnings and endings,
Growings and maturings,
To ripenesses, fruitions,
Flowings of up and down,
Increasing, decreasing,
Now blooming, now petals,
Falling from the roses,
Sunshine, cloudy, or rain,
The rhythms continue
Endlessly again and again.

MOONLIGHT ON BISHOP PARK

Wavy moonlight water,
Shining bright silver white,
Its wavy brightness
Moves back and forth
Out on the river toward
The other distant shore in sight.
The waves dance on the milky
Moonbeams from the moon
Which is bright in the black night sky
Dark blue sky and waters
Are the backdrop for the blinking
Red lights flashing dimly
In the distance of the dark night.

AUTUMN LEAVES

Caught up in the strong winds of Autumn,
The rusty colored, dried leaves
Made a high-pitched crackling sound
As they rose higher and higher
In a small funnel shaped circle.
The leaves seemed to rejoice.
Their season was now ending.
They would fall into the ground
And begin their winter hibernation.
They would make the earth fertile
For the new life of another Springtime.

DREAMS OF TOMORROW

Even when you're gone,
The eyes of the morrow,
Along that imaginary road
Keep you always on my mind.
Life is a labyrinth,
But I know that for us,
Our song of love
And our destiny
Will be fulfilled
With time and forever.
You are my everything.
The love rhymes,
And idyllic memories
Have been weaving the path
To our true happy ending.

HOW BEAUTIFUL

How beautiful is love remembered,
A love that has gone so far away,
We were so young and innocent,
But our love had already gone astray.

How beautiful is love remembered,
There was always a price to pay,
Vulnerable and open, eager to please,
Our hearts we must obey.

How beautiful is love remembered,
Kindness, goodness, and tenderness,
All have their day.
The romance and fantasy of love,
Brought us closer and made us
Want to pray.

How beautiful is love remembered,
Resplendent images and music
Brightened our way.
Such love remembered
Is more beautiful
With every passing day.

RARE MOMENTS

Like a solitary guitar playing
In the nighttime village square,
I felt myself caught up
In the lonesome melody
That played in the evening air.
I heard music that wasn't there.
Rare moods and rare feelings
Made everything in my every day
Seem unusual and unique,
Not like work but more like play,
Humble but not meek,
Bright and not bleak.

WHAT IS ETERNITY

It is one of life's greatest mysteries,
Where time and distance blend.
Eternity is forever,
Has no beginning,
Has no end.
It is the happy hunting ground,
The heavenly paradise
Where most hope to go,
But it is only after death
That we will really know.
It is more years than all the grains
Of sands on all beaches in the world,
And it is farther in distance than
The smallest star in the nighttime sky
In the endless universe unfurled.

SWEET SIXTEEN

He had been searching for his sweet sixteen.
Before the clock would strike nine,
He thought he might run out of time.
He had drifted very slowly back to his past.
While his sweet sixteen gave such a contrast.
Passion, romance, and music
Sorrow, hurt, and misunderstanding
Were all a part of this romantic dream.
He had finally come to appreciate
The simple things of life as well as
His sweet sixteen.

AUTUMN FIRST LOVE

Golden leaves flew across the ground,
Bouncing, flittering, and tossing around.
The couple watched from their park bench.
Their romantic interlude just happened.
Their young love would not be denied.
The first touch, the first kiss, the first flower,
Stolen moments, tender, quiet in the night,
Full of pleasure, wonder and joy.
Sitting on the park bench that day,
Watching the squirrels play together,
Their happiness and heavenly delight
Was something they could effortlessly enjoy.

LOST INTERVALS

Searching and looking,
Looking and searching,
Always trying to find
The part of yourself
That's been missing for a while.
It's the part of your heart
The part of your soul,
The part of your mind
That you have somehow left behind.

She knew what you were searching for.
She knew she was a part of it all.
Searching and looking,
Looking and searching
Trying very much to put it
All back together again.
The insight had been learned.
It didn't have to be
Such a struggle after all.

GRACE

So many events,
So many circumstances,
So many accidents of birth,
Are all related in a common thread.
They form the myriad picture
Of the unique person
That we are,
And that we are becoming.

POEMS OF LIFE

Every life is a complete universe,
Large, small or somewhere in between.
Various images of time and place
Recall the stages of life's scenes.
Our first memories of infancy
Begin as a state of utter dependency,
Helpless, we cry for everything.
Vague memories are like a dream.
Childhood has the most lasting effect
Though the recollections are also fuzzy;
Grade school, middle school, and high school
Seemed to go on and on forever.
In our maturity and young adulthood,
Our paths are more unlike and specific.
Poems fittingly express the diverse stories
Of the numerous phases of our lives;
Thus, we may call them the poems of life.

RAINBOWS

Magical colors of the spectrum
Reflecting the radiant sun;
All of our secret wishes
Were contained in those endless
Upstretched arcs
One by one.

Natural wonder of beauty,
The blend of orange,
Yellow, red, white and blue;
A rare and unique sight,
There was not one rainbow
But two.

CITY SNOWFALL

On the city street everything was covered
With a thick blanket of white snow,
Graceful and soft, elegant whiteness.
It was quiet now, even the traffic
Had slowed down.
There was a still, steady stream
Of snowflakes coming down,
On a slanted angle.
They were visible as one large wall
Forming a tapestry.
The numerous white snowflakes were
Set against the black darkness
As the many stars shine
Against the dark heavens at night,
Very attractive as they reflected
Off the city street lamp.

CONTEMPLATION

Round and round as my days evolve,
I contemplate some of life's puzzles
That I would solve.

I am but a single creature
Within this vast universe,
Wondering about the many mysteries
In which we are immersed.

From the simple blades of grass
Blowing gently in the breeze,
To the commanding stature
Of all the tall oak trees;

From all the many tiny white stars
That dot the nighttime sky,
Reflecting on all of this
Makes me feel more humble thereby.

WORLD TRAVELER

I have known the wonders of life,
The beauty of music
Of the day and the night,
As they would go rushing by.

I have seen the heavens
From both near and far,
Travelling hundreds of miles
By jet plane per hour.
I could look out the window
Of the huge airplane
And survey the vast expanse
Of blue sky and endless terrain.

I have journeyed far from home,
Even to Africa and beyond.
Seeing different peoples, places,
With different languages and customs
Was a privelege and a blessing
That in later years
I would fondly reflect upon.

INCOGNITO

Disguised and demure,
Fooling everyone and even themselves;
They are excited by their own cover.
With a completely different
Apppearance than usual
They are doing their job.
Enjoying their new identity.
Turned on by their temporary role.
They feel conceited as they say,
"Look at me, see how I am a new,
Different person".
Masquerading in a world of many deceits,
Feeling the intrigue of the moment,
They are incognito.

CAN I WRITE THIS POEM?

Can I write this poem?
Can I ever know the feeling
That I want to name?
Can I share the reality
With pretty metaphors
Which I want to frame?
Can I put into words
The nuances and details
In the recesses of my soul
Not often seen or heard?
Can I write this poem
For better or for worse,
In traditional rhyme
Or modern free verse?

SPRING'S AMBITION

When the breeze is warm and the rays of the sun
Beat down good-naturedly upon your face,
You can tell Spring is beginning.
The color of light green is everywhere
In the upper branches of all the trees,
The April showers nourish new flowers.
The tenseness of the cold frigid winter days,
Has been replaced by the relaxing days
Of this milder and warmer season.
A mood of new birth is in the air.
Nature gives new life and hope.

POETRY MAN

Poetry man your destiny
Has already been ordained.
You were meant to be a teacher,
A lover of words, a consummate storyteller,
Both otherworldly and mundane,
A lover of the artful phrase,
An entertainer with wit and charm,
Simple yet urbane.
You must give the impression
Of a sophisticated, self-possessed man,
Who has become wise to the ways
Of the world since time began.
You must be all to each and each to all,
Pleasing most as you compose. After all, poetry is very different from prose.

STARLIGHT REFLECTIONS

Gazing at the velvet, blue sky,
Dotted by the twinkling, white stars,
Shining so high;
My heart was filled with wonder and awe,
As I thought about the many things
Our Creator foresaw.

I was humbled at the sight
Of the universe so vast and so bright.
My life seemed small by comparison.
It was like one of the tiny stars
Blinking on and off again.

BLUE FANTASY

The yellow light
Of my evening table
Lamp burns brightly
But in my heart
I've flown away;
Far away, to the sea
Along the dark blue
Shining, silver sea.

I stand quietly
With peace and calmness
In my heart
There at the sea coast.
Looking across
The waves and blueness,
I contemplate the
Vastness and depth.

In the silence
Of my soul I wonder
How the time passes by,
And how so much
Takes place -
Deep and mysterious
As the dark, blue
Shining, silver sea.

BLUE MIST

I dreamed of a long ago time
When our love was young
And she was all mine.
So many yesterdays,
So many evenings,
So many hours,
Filled with enchantment,
Dreams and flowers.
A beautiful memory,
Grown rosy with the passing years,
Filled with such happiness
But also some tears.
I've come to exist
With only this thin blue mist
Of a past reminder

COLORFUL FIRMAMENT

The power, the beauty, and the majesty
Of the Almighty is written in the sky.
Day by day as the cloud formations
Gradually change their shapes and patterns
They present all His many colors.
Blue, white, gray, silver, pink and gold
At times flowing together or separately,
They are a mighty celebration
Of the natural resplendent perfection
And vastness of the universe.

DREAMING OF LOVE

Dreaming of someone who was sitting there
In the opposite chair,
Someone to talk to and to share,

I was dreaming of someone to walk with,
To share the simple beauty of nature,
And the visible world,
And yet I usually walked alone.

I had dreamed of a night in Summer,
When I was standing by the river,
With her by my side.
All the city lights reflected
On the dark, mildlly wavy waters
Giving the river a fluid, shiny look.

We had known the excitement
And joy of being together,
And of being in love.

EARLY MORNING STILLNESS

With the stillness and peace
Of the early morning hours
Long before the sun rises,
And sheds its wondrous light
On all the many flowers:

While sitting alone quietly
In a well-lit place,
There is time to pause
And meditate
On the many realities
That all of us must
Eventually face.

EDGE OF A FANTASY

On the edge of a fantasy,
Quickly we run from reality,
In leaps and bounds.
We are searching
For our own unique happiness.
Imagining and wishing,
Desiring the best of dreams,
Remembering the secret hopes
And all the well-planned schemes,
Never knowing exactly,
How our story
Would finally unfold.
Eager hearts are always loving,
Always yearning for their fantasy
To behold.

FLOWER OF NEW LOVE

Her smile was like a flower in bloom,
The fragrance of her new found love
Softly flowed forth as sweet perfume.

Rose petals descended one by one,
And a tulip bud began to slowly open
As in Spring is done.

The beauty of her fair and comely face
Had left a flower-like impression
On his heart
That time would not erase.

AUTUMN BREEZE

Whisper softly autumn breeze
Through the rustle of the leaves,
Tell me something if you please.

My heart has grown weary
With the passing of the years.
So, autumn breeze, lift my spirits.
Tell me some stories of my past
With all the laughter and the tears.

Pure fresh light air,
And the slight coolness
That you possess,
Autumn breeze bring me hope
For a happier tomorrow
Wih some love and tenderness.

THE HAUNTED BACHELOR

His nights were filled with voices,
Voices of pretty ladies,
Standing outside his door.
"Am I good enough?" they would ask
"Or how about me?" another would say.
It made him wonder, if he opened the door
Would they really be there?
His imagination gave them an alluring
And seductive quality. Roses, perfume,
Tenderness, warmth and caring; all the good
Side of love and romance came to his mind.
He continued to wonder.

NATURAL IMPRESSIONS

Orange, yellow, gold, green, red
Blue, white and brown
Are some of the lively colors
That are present in the natural
Scene all around.

A profusion of shades and hues
Are readily available in the sky
With its wondrous patterns of clouds
Or its many sunrisings or sunsets
That regularly please our eyes.

Cool, gentle breezes blowing softly
In the summertime
Turn the leaves in the trees
Into flickering green and white lights
As they toss back and forth
Effortlessly keeping rhythmical time.

LILAC MAGIC

In the early morning hours
At the dawn of a new day,
The sky is colored with a lilac light.

And on the grassy paths
Out on the countryside
The morning dew has a lilac sheen.

Among all the many blossoms
And vegeation there are also
The radiant lilac flowers.

Smooth and gentle,
Light and clear,
The natural beauty of lilac
Or light purple, is always near.

Lilac twilight and lilac evening
Colors the lilac horizon.
Then comes the dark blue
Of nighttime.

LISTEN TO THE WAVES

Ocean waves washing up along the shore,
The relaxing cadence and the easy rhythm,
It makes us wish for more.
What are the waves telling us
Amidst their gentle roar?
They are carrying many messages of wisdom,
Which are sometimes not so easy to ignore.
Calmness, peacefulness, all come in their time,
Along with tranquility evermore
We need only stop and heed the messages of wisdom
That are daily washed up along the shore.

DREAM COME TRUE

Soul reaching out to another kindred soul,
Each existing in the physical world,
They were carefully observing how
Their mutual desire would finally grow.

Their prayers and thought images
Had often expressed themselves the same way.
It was a powerful feeling of drawing closer
And uniting themselves day by day.

Flowers, fragrances, sights and sounds,
Were somehow all exciting and brand new,
And their warm closeness and love
Had made their dream come true.

LOVE FANTASY

We had been building castles in the air,
Dreaming a bridge of dreams,
Where we could cross over and enjoy a journey
Of unreality and happy adventures together.
Time had stood still for us
While we lived the dreamy highlife,
Tripping the light fantastic through yesterdays,
Todays, tomorrows as we felt the bliss
And other good feelings of our love fantasy.

LOVE IS NEVER A CLICHE

Although the subject of love
Is in all the music we hear today,
It doesn't necessarily mean
That love is just a cliche.

And even if "love" is on the TV
And soap operas each day,
The freshness and beauty of love
Never becomes a mere cliche.

Either love or experience
The vacuum of negative decay.
Love is nature's way
Of telling us how to live
With health and happiness always.

Like the air we breathe
And the food we eat,
Love is vital and basic.
It is never simply a cliche.

LOVE OPENS EVERY DOOR

There is a positive goodness that we can rarely ignore
It is the positive power of love that opens every door.

Man's humanity to man is the ideal of evermore,
Instead God's peace and justice is what each day
We finally must implore.

In the beauty of springtime all hearts turn to love
which sometimes may be in store,
As love's fascination draws us all to its romantic reservoir.

Life requires struggle with opposition and a knowing
of the score,
A striving for a balance and a moderation, and a harmony
of once more.

Love conquers all, so it is frequently told in many books
of yore,
It is another reminder that the positive force of love
really does open every door.

LOVE PORTRAIT

She is the magic.
She is the music, the words,
And the symphony
She is everything to me.

Once a voice told me,
"If you really love her,
Then let her be free.
If she really loves you,
She will return, since
She will always wish
Your company."

She is my whole world
She is all my poetry.
She is in my every fantasy.

When I recall her sweet smile,
Everything feels worthwhile.

MARIA AND THE MOON

It was warm that evening, and not quite June,
When Maria and I drove down by the river
To see the big, yellow full moon.
She was talking and laughing,
Apparently in a good mood.
So too, the big yellow moon likewise
Seemed happy and cheerful too.
The big, yellow, pale moon suspended
In the dark nighttime sky,
Made me imagine many different,
Faraway places, times and lives.
How did this moon look over Vienna,
Athens or Rome?
Somehow it must be a little different
Than the one Maria and I
Were seeing here at home.

MEDITATION

Moments of peace have more meaning.
Times of stillness give us a gleaning,
A glimpse of fullness,
And the colors of feelings.
Blue, green and gold thoughts, gently streaming
Without any effort for you to hold.

More and more learning about the other side
Of yourself and being;
A gentle flowing of all your senses
Which are sensing your foreverness,
For a little while.

MEMENTOS

Pretty flowers tumbling through the air,
She is their fragrance and their face so fair.
The music, the candle, and the wine
She also brings all of these to mind.

It feels like such a long time ago,
That she was his girl and he was her beau.
In his dreams she keeps returning to him
As his lonesome heart is looking grim.

She is sometimes in the wind that blows
No matter what the season,
Then again, she appears sometimes
In the daylight, or the moonlight
For no apparent reason.

Gazing on all the many flowers tumbling down,
He wondered at how time goes by and how a heart
Can feel love that is so profound.

MIDNIGHT RHAPSODIES

The music flows through the night air.
It is playing on the airwaves of radios.
Flowing in all directions, everywhere.
The seductive sounds evoke images
Of old dreams and memories.
As the music plays on, my imagination
Wanders to thoughts of love, romances,
And traveling to exotic places.
All the memories grow fonder
As the melody ebbs and flows easily,
So do my moods and feelings,
As in a rhapsody.

THE MYSTIC

Mystical man, many are they
Who come and go.
His mystery sets him apart
From all the rest, apropos.
Whenever he enters a room
It creates a stir.
People anticipate that
Something magical might occur.
Unusual phenomena that are
Difficult to explain,
Sometimes happen as long
As he remains.
He is in touch with the
Supernatural, so people say,
But his gifts just keep on coming
They don't go away.

MYSTIC AVENUES

Winding along, leading on to the next
Enchanted cross street, and far beyond,
Mystic avenues with a meandering way,
Proceeding to a certain destination,
In an uncertain future place.
Just imagine as you are driving;
And the day is drawing to an end.
The headlights of the cars riding
Back and forth grow stronger,
Shining their bright beams of light
Into the recesses and crooks,
Giving the avenues their mysterious
And inscrutable look.

NIGHT WISH

Sweetness of my life,
Come to me tonight.
Help me rest my weariness,
Refresh me with your tenderness.
We'll talk, we'll laugh,
And be at ease.
We will relax together
And do what we please.
How simple it all seems,
And yet it's only in my dreams.
So sweetness of my life,
Come to me tonight.
Let's make some
Beautiful memories together.

OUR CREATOR

Oh Ineffable Trinity,
Father, Son and Holy Spirit,
The Uncreated Source
Of all creation,
We acknowledge your
Almighty power, wisdom,
And love for your creatures,
Our finite minds cannot begin
To appreciate all your many qualities
Of omniscience, omnipresence, and
Omnipotence Dear Father God,
Manifest in your wondrous creation.
We must pray each day to understand
And to know better through faith
Your profound mystery.

POEM OF BEAUTY

Poem of beauty, poem of light,
Tell me a story, make everything right.

Poem of beauty, poem of love,
Bring me quiet peace, send the white dove.

Poem of beauty, poem of truth,
Show me some errors of my foolish youth.

Poem of beauty, poem of song,
Tell me the verses so I may sing along.

Poem of beauty, poem of rhyme,
Tell me a bit of history, tell it in time.

Poem of beauty, poem of light,
Shed your goodness upon me.
Grant me some sweet dreams this night.

POEM SONG

A poem as enchanting as a song
It was written there all along.

My heart knew the beauty and the love,
The golden inspiration which comes from above.

My couplets were in perfect rhyme
While the lyrics pertained to all of time.

Capturing the new mood in a simple fresh way
Seemed to come to me day after day.

My hope was that the music would shine through
With every poem that I would write anew.

REMEMBERING

Remembering far back,
Once long ago,
When I was youthful
And had a need to know.

All of life
Filled me with awe,
And I remained charmed
By all that I saw.

As I wandered along
Going here and there,
I felt deep down
That God was just
And fair.

REVERIE

Will our paths ever cross again?
If so, I wonder when?
What does destiny hold in store,
If we should ever see each other once more?
Many years have already passed
Since the days of our youthful love
That we thought would always last.
Hoping against hope and dreaming
The impossible dream.
Trying to imagine what it would be like;
That first uncertain scene.
Winter, fall, summer, and spring,
The seasons slowly pass away,
As I continue wondering
If we'll ever have our day.

FOR HEAVEN

Surrounded by fantasies,
We are dreamers,
Trying to live out
Our desires, wishes and hopes.

We are all fellow travelers
Struggling, sometimes, even
Stumbling along our way
To a destination
That is not always clear.

Our eternal Father calls us
In many different, individual ways,
If we would only listen.
He calls us to our everlasting
Home, our birthright,
The longing of our soul
Which is heaven.

SAYING GOODBYE

The journey back in time
Came in those lonely moments
While sitting by the river
On warm summer evenings.
The persistence of memory
Recalled that farewell
From distant harbors,
And faraway lands.
In our shared visions we had
Pushed the clouds away.
Many joys and many sorrows
Had come and gone.
Our friendship was ending.
We would go our separate ways.
Saying goodbye was not always easy.

SOARING SPIRITS

Piano and violin
Together blend
And fill our hearts
With pleasant joy.
While above us
In the velvet
Blue starry sky
Our spirits
Have gone to fly.

STAY WITH ME ALWAYS

Starlight of my every evening,
Sunshine of my every day,
You have made me very happy,
Stay with me always, stay.

Like the flowers in the garden
Blooming in the first days of May,
You came into my quiet life,
Stay with me always, stay.

You make me feel more fulfilled
In each and every little way,
So, it's natural that I'm asking
Stay with me always, stay.

If we always remain together,
And this is what I earnestly pray,
Every tomorrow will be brighter,
So, stay with me always, stay.

STRANDED IN TIME

Caught up in this earthly life,
Not knowing where the beginning
Or the ending came,
He was just in a pending status.

One day, he woke up.
And it all occurred to him
In a few seconds as a flash
Of insight.

Somehow he had been slowly
Moving right into a standstill.
Everyone else was still moving
Forward or backward or sideways,
But he had stopped.

TIME AND FOREVER

There is a forever in every moment
When we live our lives with that special
Consciousness and awareness.
Minutes last for hours,
And it is a joy to be alive,
We have to become more simple,
More concentrated, more focused.
Yet our daily routines do not always
Allow us to do so.
Moment after moment they go,
Always passing away into forever.
If only we could catch a moment
And live it more fully,
We could make our personal hour-glass
More full of time and forever.

TWILIGHT BLUE

When the bright golden sun
Begins to set
And the light blue sky
Blends with the rosy violet.

Nature reminds us
It is almost day's end.
We must now make ready
Our activities to suspend.

So many days like this
Have come and gone
We always believe
There will be another dawn.

And yet the special beauty
Of the twilight blue
Regrettably is only noticed
By a very few.

TWO HEARTS

When two hearts met,
They fell in love.
They had no regret.

Their two hearts sang
And danced and laughed,
And soon, wedding bells rang.

Their two hearts beat
Together as one.
And then, a third heart
Was born, and a life begun.

The miracle of two hearts
In love is full of wonder.
It is a lesson for us all
To remember and to ponder.

WORDS OF LOVE

Words of love,
Travel through the years,
Echoing the laughter,
Echoing the tears.

Words of love,
Demonstrate the many measures,
Reflecting the simple joys,
Reflecting the routine pleasures.

Words of love,
Recall the many enchanted hours,
Walking in the summer sunshine,
Walking in the fragrance of fresh flowers.

Words of love,
Sometimes resemble a dream,
Capturing days of rare beauty,
Capturing summer nights serene.

Words of love,
Describe two souls in love sincere,
Echoing their laughter,
Echoing their tears.

WHEN PATHS CROSS

Our eye contact reminds us
Of the secret struggles
We experience
Within our souls.

Serious thoughts reflected
Upon our faces demonstrate
The unspoken conflicts
That we are living.

Morning, noon, and nighttime,
We go through an ordinary day,
We meet our fellow travelers
Who are also attempting
The pursuit of their
Own unique way.

A casual word, a glance,
Or even a smile,
Manifests the hidden, underlying,
Personal drama unfolding;
All the yearning and striving,
To achieve our uncertain destinies.

COURAGE

Dare to follow your heart's desire.
Life, after all, never asks of us
Any more than that which is required.

Don't be discouraged if things don't always
Turn out just so.
Sometimes your mistakes are just as important
As the things you already know.

Never lose sight of your final goal.
Remember, the parts are equally as significant
As the whole.

Courage is something we all must maintain.
We must always be willing to pick up
And keep going again.

A POEM A DAY

Write me a poem each day.
Write all the things you want to say.

Write some beautiful words.
Add the hidden music that will also be heard.

Write the feelings and moods.
With metaphors and similes that are shrewd.

A poem a day is very good so they say,
Sometimes it helps to chase the blues away.

About the Author

Gilbert Saenz (Pen Name: Gil Saenz) was born in Detroit, Michigan on October 17, 1941. His parents are Valentine and Lena Saenz (both now deceased). He is employed as a Computer Specialist with the government. He received his B.A. in English Literature in June, 1968 at Wayne State University, Detroit, Michigan.

In addition, he has completed two years of post-degree studies also at Wayne State University. From 1960 to 1963 he worked as a Personnel Specialist in the United States Air Force. He has also served as a U.S. Diplomatic Courier in the Foreign Service at the Frankfurt, Germany office from 1969 to 1970.

Gil began publishing poems in 1984. To date he has published over two-hundred-seventy of his poems individually. Also, he has published five collections of his own poems which are entitled as follows: *Where Love Is* (88), *Colorful Impressions* (93), *Moments In Time* (95), *Lavender and Lace* co-authored with Jacqueline Sanchez (98), *Dreaming of Love* (99), and *Poems of Life/Poemas de la vida* (01). Gil is a member of the Detroit area Latino Poets Association and the Downriver Poets and Playwrights in Wyandotte, Michigan. He is also a member of the Poetry Society of Michigan and the Academy of American Poets. Some of his favorite themes include: love, romance, nature, beauty, and the spiritual-religious. "Poetry is an excellent way of expressing ideas, moods, and feelings which may not usually be expressed in other ways."

OTHER POETRY BOOKS BY GIL SAENZ

WHERE LOVE IS
Second Printing
Minnesota Ink, Inc., 1988
St. Paul, Minnesota

COLORFUL IMPRESSIONS
Printed by Casa De Unidad, 1993
Detroit, Michigan

MOMENTS IN TIME
Printed by
Bookmasters, Inc., 1995
Ashland, Ohio

LAVENDER & LACE
Co-Authored with Jacqueline Sanchez
Published by
Sounds of Poetry, 1998
Detroit, Michigan

DREAMING OF LOVE
Published by
Pentland Press, Inc., 1999
Raleigh, North Carolina

POEMS OF LIFE/POEMAS DE LA VIDA
Published by
Laredo Publishing Co., 2001
Beverly Hills, California

CPSIA information can be obtained
at www.ICGtesting.com
Printed in the USA
LVHW050836200122
708837LV00011B/731

9 781685 360337